100 MORE ACTION SONGS!

FOR PRESCHOOLERS

We wish to thank these people for their help in this project:
Deborah Berkimer
Karen Brigham
Robin Currie
Jeanette Dall
Carl Heine
Amy and Rebekah Hill
Neta Jackson
Lois Keffer
Debbie Powell
Donald and Brenda Ratcliff
Laurie Riddle
Janet Southern
Anna Trimiew
Ramona Warren

100 MORE ACTION SONGS FOR PRESCHOOLERS

© 1991 by David C. Cook Publishing Co.

Designed by Christopher Patchel and Elizabeth Thompson
Printed in the United States of America

ISBN: 1-55513-456-4

CONTENTS

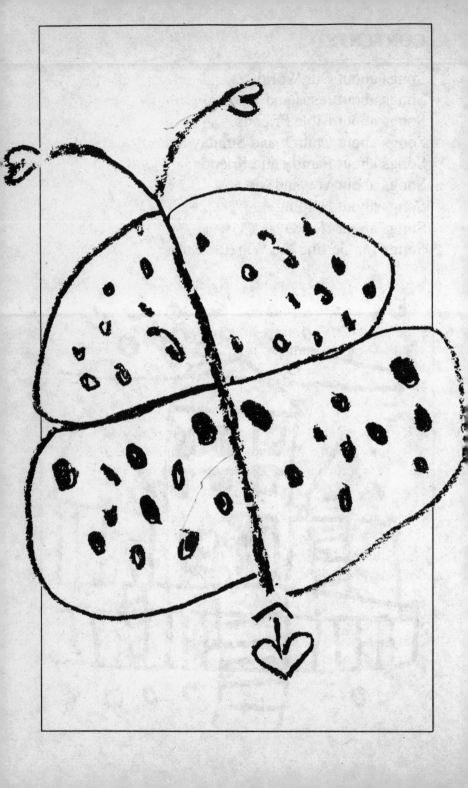

OUR WORLD

1 Let children celebrate the wonderful world God has made as they clap and sing this song to the tune of *The Farmer in the Dell*.

God gave us a wonderful world.
God gave us a wonderful world.
Let's all thank Him for this gift.
God gave us a wonderful world.

These next few songs list some of the specific things God has made.

2 Clap and sing this to the tune of *Row, Row, Row Your Boat*:

Plants, plants, God made plants.
He made all the plants.
We need plants to help us live.
Praise God for the plants.

3 Try to find a picture of each animal mentioned in this song. Hand out pictures and have children hold them up at the appropriate time in the song. Sing to *Paw-Paw Patch*.

God made lions, God made raccoons.
God made dolphins, cats, and baboons.
God made birds to sing lots of tunes.
God made animals for me and you.

God made chicks and kangaroos.
God made zebras, dogs, and moose.
God made spiders, penguins, too.
God made animals for me and you.

4 To *Skip to My Lou:*

God made the fish.
  Make swimming motions
And God made the seas.
God made the birds.
  Make flying motions
And God made the trees.
God made you,
  Point to someone
And God made me.
  Point to self
God made it all.
  Spread arms out
Let's praise Him!
  Clap hands

5 Have children hold hands and sway as they sing this song to *Did You Ever See a Lassie?*

Did you ever see the oceans,
The oceans, the oceans.
Did you know God made the oceans?
He made them just right.

Add other verses, substituting words such as **"a mountain," "a pear tree," "a parrot," "a zebra," "a snowflake,"** and so on for the words **"the oceans."**

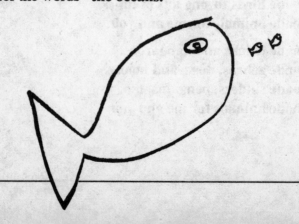

6 Teach preschoolers this song which will help them review the creation story. Use motions when appropriate and sing to the tune of *The Farmer in the Dell*.

God said, "I'll make the world." *(Repeat)*
God said it and the world was made.
God said, "I'll make the world."

God said, "Let there be light." *(Repeat)*
God said it and the light was made.
God said, "Let there be light."

vs. 3   **God said, "I'll make the sky."**
vs. 4   **God said, "I'll make the seas."**
vs. 5   **God said, "I'll make the plants."**
vs. 6   **God said, "I'll make the sun."**
vs. 7   **God said, "I'll make the moon."**
vs. 8   **God said, "I'll make the stars."**
vs. 9   **God said, "I'll make the fish."**
vs. 10   **God said, "I'll make the birds."**
vs. 11   **God said, "I'll make the animals."**
vs. 12   **God said, "I'll make a man."**

7 Here's another creation song to the tune of *Good Night, Ladies*.

God made green trees. *(Repeat 2x)*
  Pretend to be a tree
I'm glad God made the trees.

God made big whales. *(Repeat 2x)*
  Pretend to be a whale
I'm glad God made the whales.

God made people. *(Repeat 2x)*
  Point to each other
I'm glad that God made me.

God made all things. *(Repeat 2x)*
  Hold arms out to the side
I'm glad God made all things.

JESUS AND GOD

8 *I've Been working on the Railroad* is the tune for this song about Jesus' care.

I'm so glad that Jesus loves me,
  Point up then to self
He helps me each day.
I'm so glad that Jesus loves me,
  Point up then to self
And He never goes away.
  Shake head, "no"
When I'm sad or when I'm lonely,
  Show expressions
When I feel okay—
Jesus loves me and protects me
  Hug self
Every single day.

9 Children will enjoy helping to make up verses for this next song sung to *The Farmer in the Dell*. Have them point to the things they sing about.

God gives us many things.
God gives us many things.
He gives us all the things we need.
God gives us many things.

The flowers and the trees.
The flowers and the trees.
God gives us all the things we need.
The flowers and the trees.

10 Sing the verses of the song to *Skip to My Lou*. Do the actions indicated. Add other verses by using different actions for the word **"clap"** such as **"march," "jump," "hop,"** and **"shout."**

I love Jesus, yes, I do.
I love Jesus, yes, I do.
I love Jesus, yes, I do.
I love to sing and praise Him.

I love to praise Him with a clap. *(Repeat 2 x)*
I love to sing and praise Him.

11 *Mary Had a Little Lamb* is the tune for this next song.

Are you sick, alone, or sad?
Jesus cares, Jesus cares.
   Point up on the word Jesus
Are you sick, alone, or sad?
Jesus cares for you.
   Point up then to a person

12 *The Mulberry Bush* is the tune for this next song. Have preschoolers clap as they sing the first verse.

Jesus is my special friend,
Special friend, special friend.
I can do things Jesus did.
He is my special friend.

I can pray like Jesus did,
Like Jesus did, like Jesus did.
I can pray like Jesus did.
  Bow heads and fold hands
He is my special friend.
  Point up then hug self

I can tell of Jesus' love,
Jesus' love, Jesus' love.
  Point to mouth then up
I can tell of Jesus' love.
He is my special friend.
  Point up then hug self

13 Teach preschoolers this song to the tune of *I'm a Little Teapot*.

Jesus is my best friend
  Point up
Yes, indeed!
  Shake head, "yes"
He takes care of all my needs.
When I am afraid He comforts me.
  Hug self
Jesus is my best friend
  Point up
Yes, indeed!
  Shake head, "yes"

14 Children will enjoy this song which has a different set of actions for each verse. Sing to the tune of *The Muffin Man*.

Stand in a circle and clap to rhythm of words as you sing:
The children of God needed help,
Needed help, needed help.
The children of God needed help,
To cross the big Red Sea.

Make sweeping hand motions to show (deep) and (wide):
The water was deep, the water was wide,
Deep and wide, deep and wide.
The water was deep, the water was wide.
How could they get across?

Do the actions mentioned in this next verse:
Did they jump or swim or fly . . .
Swim or fly, swim or fly?
Did they jump or swim or fly?
How did they get across?

Pretend to blow and sway from side to side. Show path with hands:
God blew the water from side to side,
Side to side, side to side.
God blew the water from side to side.
So they could get across.

March in a circle and clap as you sing:
They walked across like a big parade,
A big parade, a big parade.
They walked across like a big parade.
God helped them get across.

15 Lead children in doing the motions for this next song sung to the tune of *The Farmer in the Dell*.

Form roof over head with hands as you sing:
God gives me a place to live. *(Repeat)*
A happy place that I call home,
God gives me a place to live.

Extend arms as if to hug family as you sing:
God gives me a family. *(Repeat)*
They always take good care of me,
God gives me a family.

Pretend to throw a ball and then sweep with a broom as you sing:
We play and work together. *(Repeat)*
Thank You, God, for every day,
We play and work together.

Jump up and down and clap as you sing:
We praise God for our homes. *(Repeat)*
It's good to have a place to live.
We praise God for our homes.

16 Sing this song to the tune of *Oh, Be Careful*. Have children stand in a circle and clap to the rhythm of the words, or march around in a circle.

God gives us everything that we need.
God gives us everything that we need.
We have a place to stay.
We live at home each day.
God gives us everything that we need.

For more verses substitute these lines for the last three of verse one:

vs. 2   **Our friends are happy here.**
          And we're glad to have them near.
          God gives us everything that we need.

vs. 3   **He listens as we speak,**
          And He helps us every week.
          God gives us everything that we need.

vs. 4   **We listen to Him say,**
          "Obey My rules today."
          God gives us everything that we need.

17 While singing this song let children call out ways Jesus shows His love for them at the end of each verse. Sing to the tune of *The Mulberry Bush*.

Jesus shows His love for me
   Point to the sky
Every day, every day.
   Cross arms over chest
Jesus shows His love for me
   Point to the sky
In this special way.
   Shake finger in rhythm

18 For this song, have children join hands and move around in a circle. On the last line, stop and raise up hands, as if pointing to God. Sing to the tune of *The Mulberry Bush.*

Every time we sing God's praise,
Sing God's praise, sing God's praise,
Every time we sing God's praise,
We show our love to Him.

Every time we thank our God,
Thank our God, thank our God,
Every time we thank our God,
We show our love to Him.

Every time that we obey,
We obey, we obey,
Every time that we obey,
We show our love to Him.

Every time we trust God's care,
Trust God's care, trust God's care,
Every time we trust God's care,
We show our love to Him.

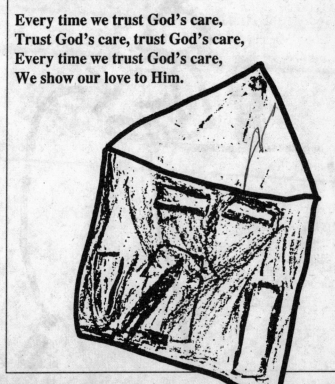

BIBLE FRIENDS

19 Preschoolers will be reminded of God's care for them by singing these words to the tune of *The Mulberry Bush*. They may enjoy circling around as they sing the first three lines, then stopping and pointing to self on the last line.

**God took care of Moses' friends,
Moses' friends, Moses' friends.
God took care of Moses' friends,
And God will care for me.**

**God took care of Abraham,
Abraham, Abraham.
God took care of Abraham,
And God will care for me.**

20 Teach these words about Peter and John to the tune of *The Mulberry Bush*.

Pretend to walk as you sing:
**Peter and John met a man
Met a man, met a man.
Peter and John met a man
On their way to church.**

Sit and put on a sad face as you sing:
**The man just sat—he could not walk
Could not walk, could not walk.
The man just sat—he could not walk.
He was so very sad.**

Stand and motion to the sick man as you sing:
**Peter and John said, "Rise and walk,
Rise and walk, rise and walk."
Peter and John said, "Rise and walk
In Jesus' name today."**

Imitate the man walking happily as you sing:
**The man stood up and walked around
Walked around, walked around.
The man stood up and walked around.
He was so very happy!**

21 These words to *Twinkle, Twinkle, Little Star* tell of some of Jesus' miracles. Add actions where appropriate.

**Bartimaeus could not see.
Ten men were sick with leprosy.
One was lame and couldn't walk.
One was deaf; one couldn't talk.
Jesus healed them every one
For He was God's only Son.**

22

Review some of the characters of the Old Testament by singing this song to *Are You Sleeping?*

Where is Noah, where is Noah?
Here I am. Here I am.
  Point to self
I will build the ark.
  Pretend to build
I will build the ark.
I'll obey, I'll obey.
  Point to self

Where is Moses, where is Moses?
Here I am. Here I am.
  Point to self
I will lead your people.
  Pretend to walk
I will lead your people.
I'll obey, I'll obey.
  Point to self

Where is Jonah, where is Jonah?
Here I am. Here I am.
  Point to self
I will warn the people.
  Put hand up to mouth
I will warn the people.
I'll obey, I'll obey.
  Point to self

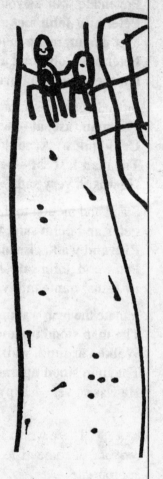

Where are the children? Where are the children?
Here we are. Here we are.
  Spread out arms
We will follow Jesus.
  Shake head, "yes"
We will follow Jesus.
We'll obey, We'll obey.

23

Adapt *Old MacDonald Had a Farm* and teach these words that tell about Noah. Add as many animals as you'd like.

Noah sailed his great big ark
   Hold two hands together and move like a boat going through water
Forty days and nights.
And on the ark he had two cows,
   Hold up two fingers
Forty days and nights.
With a moo-moo here, and a moo-moo there,
   Turn head to right then to left
Here a moo, there a moo,
Everywhere a moo-moo.
   Spread arms out
Noah sailed his great big ark
Forty days and nights.

24

Sing this song to *Baa, Baa, Black Sheep*.

Little lost sheep, tell me where you are.
   Put hand to eyes as if looking for the sheep
Please don't wander very far.
It is dark and very cold.
   Hug self and shiver
Please come back into the fold.
   Move hand towards self as if motioning someone to come

CHURCH AND SUNDAY SCHOOL

25 This song will remind children to be thankful for leaders that work in their churches. Follow the actions and sing to *Jim Crack Corn*.

Praise the Lord and walk around, *(Repeat 2x)*
For leaders in our church.

Praise the Lord and clap your hands, *(Repeat 2x)*
For teachers in our church.

Praise the Lord and jump right up, *(Repeat 2x)*
For the pastor in our church.

Praise the Lord and la-la-la, *(Repeat 2x)*
   Cup hands around mouth on "la-la-la"
For the choir director in our church.

Repeat first verse again.

26 Have preschoolers clap as they sing this action song to the tune of *If You're Happy*.

If you love the Lord your God with all your heart, say I do! *(Repeat)*
You can worship God today,
Singing songs will help you say,
That you love the Lord your God with all your heart.

Substitute these lines for the third line above:

Bringing gifts will help you say . . .
Offering prayers will help you say . . .
Clapping hands will help you say . . .
Shouting praise will help you say . . .

27 Children will enjoy learning this good-bye song to the tune of *Did You Ever See a Lassie?*

On this first verse, children stand in a circle while leader stands in the middle. On other verses a child can be invited to stand in the middle with the leader.

Now it's time to say good-bye, good-bye, good-bye,
Now it's time to say good-bye, good-bye to our friends.
Wave to this friend and that friend,
  Children wave to each other
And this friend and that friend.
Now it's time to say good-bye, good-bye to our friends.

vs. 2   **Now it's time to give a hug, a hug, a hug,**

vs. 3   **Next week we'll get together, together, together,**
Next week we'll get together, together with friends.
With this friend and that friend,
  Children point to each other
And this friend and that friend.
Next week we'll get together, together with friends.

28 Use this song to prepare children for the Bible lesson of the day. It is sung to *This Old Man*.

Listening ears, listening ears,
  Cup hands behind one ear then the other
We've all got our listening ears.
  Cup hands behind both ears
We will listen to the Word of God today,
Hear it and then go obey.

29 Lead children in this song about prayer sung to the tune of *This Old Man*.

We can pray
Every day!
God will hear us when we say,
  Fold hands
"Bless my family and thank You for my food.
God is great and God is good."

We can pray
Every day!
Here or there or far away.
  Fold hands
"Thank You, God, for going with me everywhere.
Thank You for your loving care."
  Hug self

30 Teach children about giving through this song, sung to *The Bear Went Over the Mountain*.

Raise hands, palms up as you sing:
We bring our offering to church, *(Repeat 2x)*
Because we love our God.

Pretend to give an offering as you sing:
We give our offering to worship, *(Repeat 2x)*
Because we love our God.

31 Preschoolers will enjoy marching with a partner as they sing these words to *Row, Row, Row Your Boat*.

Sing, sing, sing to God
Praise Him for this day.
Happily, happily, happily, happily
Praise Him for this day.

32 Use this song to the tune of *B-I-N-G-O* to remind children to thank God for His blessings.

I know that Jesus loves us all,
So I will thank and praise Him.
  Have children clap out the rhythm as they sing this next
    line
T-H-A-N-K, T-H-A-N-K, T-H-A-N-K,
So I will thank and praise Him.

33 This next song will remind children that God hears them when they pray. It is sung to *The Mulberry Bush*.

Jesus hears us when we pray,
When we pray, when we pray.
  Cup hand behind ear; make praying hands
Jesus hears us when we pray.
We can pray today.

Jesus hears when _____(child's name) **prays,**
  Cup hand behind ear; make praying hands.
_____(child's name) **prays,** _____(child's name) **prays,**
Jesus hears when _____ (child's name) **prays,**
Each and every day.

Let's thank God for answered prayer,
  Point up; make praying hands
Answered prayer, answered prayer.
Let's thank God for answered prayer,
  Point up; make praying hands
We can thank Him now.

34 Lead children into the activities of the day by singing this song to *Twinkle, Twinkle, Little Star*.

Hello! How are you today?
Would you like to come and play?
We will sing and play with toys,
With the other girls and boys.
We will have a lot of fun!
Jesus loves us, every one!

35 Preschoolers will enjoy doing the motions for this next action song which is sung to *Mary Had a Little Lamb*.

Stand in a circle and clap hands as you sing:
Little children, praise the Lord,
Praise the Lord, praise the Lord.
Little children, praise the Lord,
Praise the Lord today.

vs. 2 Open hands, palms facing up for the word "Bible":
Praise Him for the Bible . . .

vs. 3 Make a triangle—raise arms, hands together, fingers pointing up—for steeple:
Praise Him for the children's church . . .

vs. 4 Pretend to give an offering:
Praise Him with our offerings . . .

vs. 5 Children hold hands and move around in a circle:
Little children, praise the Lord,
Praise the Lord, praise the Lord.
Little children, praise the Lord,
Praise Him every day.

36 *The Itsy Bitsy Spider* is the tune for these words.

The Bible says God loves us,
    Hold hands together to look like an open book
He hears our every prayer.
    Cup hand behind ear
We praise His name because we know He really cares.
    Hug self
We try to love each other; we're learning to forgive.
    Each child holds another child's hand
For we want to be like Jesus.
Yes! That's the way to live.
    Shake head, "yes"

37 Have children hold hands with a partner and sway as they sing this song as an invitation to prayer time. Sing it to *London Bridge*.

Lord, I like to talk to You,
Talk to You, talk to You.
Lord, I like to talk to You,
When I pray.

I love You for all You do,
All You do, all You do.
I love You for all You do
For me each day.

Bless my friends and neighbors, too,
Neighbors, too, neighbors, too.
Bless my friends and neighbors, too,
And guide their way.

38 Lead children around the room as you sing this song to *The Farmer in the Dell*.

Come worship now with me.
Come worship now with me.
We'll have fun and worship, too.
Come worship now with me.

39 This song tells of things we do at church. Children will enjoy clapping to the rhythm of this song sung to the tune *She'll Be Comin' Round the Mountain*.

We will learn of Jesus when we come to church. *(Repeat)*
We will learn that Jesus loves us. *(Repeat)*
We will learn of Jesus when we come to church.

vs. 2 **We will read the Bible when we come to church.** *(Repeat)*
We will read that Jesus loves us. *(Repeat)*
We will read the Bible when we come to church.

vs. 3 **We will pray together when we come to church.** *(Repeat)*
We will pray for one another. *(Repeat)*
We will pray together when we come to church.

40 Have children fold their hands as they sing these word to *Twinkle, Twinkle, Little Star*.

When I talk to God I say
"Dear God, help me to obey;
Help me learn to share my toys
With the other girls and boys."
When I talk to God I say,
"Dear God, help me to obey."

41

Go In and Out of the Window is the tune for this next song. Have children divide up into groups of four and join hands. Each of these small groups will circle around during the first part of the song, then move to the center on the last line.

Let's worship God together, *(Repeat 3x)*
And offerings gladly bring.

Let's tell Him that we're thankful, *(Repeat 3x)*
And joyful praises sing.

Let's show Him that we love Him; *(Repeat 3x)*
He gave us everything.

Let's tell the world about Him, *(Repeat 3x)*
For He's our heavenly King.

FAMILY AND FRIENDS

42 This song will remind children to be thankful for their families. Have them clap and sing to the tune of *Jingle Bells*.

Thank You, God; thank You, God,
For my family.
Mother, father, sister, brother,
That You gave to me.

Grandmas, grandpas, uncles, aunts,
Lots of cousins, too.
For this happy family,
Dear God, I do thank You!

43 Sing these words to the tune of *Did You Ever See a Lassie?*

Oh, I really love my family, my family, my family.
   Point to self, hug self, and sway
Oh, I really love the family that God gave to me;
   Point to self, hug self, point up, and to self
My father and mother and sister and brother.
   Hold up fingers for each person
Oh, I really love the family that God gave to me.
   Point to self, hug self, point up, and to self

44 You may need some old hats for preschoolers to wear during the different verses of this song. boys can wear men's hats during the "daddy" verse and girls can wear ladies' hats during the "mommy" verse. Sing to the tune of *The Muffin Man.*

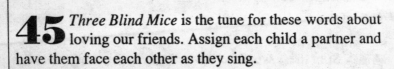

Families are a gift from God,
A gift from God, a gift from God.
Families are a gift from God,
Who gives us all good things.

vs. 2 **Daddies are a gift from God.**
vs. 3 **Mommies are a gift from God.**

45 *Three Blind Mice* is the tune for these words about loving our friends. Assign each child a partner and have them face each other as they sing.

We can love. We can love.
All of our friends, all of our friends.
We can forgive them, and we can share.
Oh, when we are friendly, they'll know we care.
Jesus loves us so much that there's love to spare.
Yes, we can love.

46 For the first verse of this song, sung to *The Mulberry Bush*, children walk around in a circle holding hands.

We are in a circle of friends,
A circle of friends, a circle of friends.
We are in a circle of friends,
Doodle-lee, doodle-lee, doo!

Children point to themselves then to a friend as they sing:
God loves me and God loves you,
God loves you, God loves you.
God loves me and God loves you,
Doodle-lee, doodle-lee, doo!

Children hug friends standing next to them and sing:
I can hug you when you're sad,
When you're sad, when you're sad.
I can hug you when you're sad.
Doodle-lee, doodle-lee, doo!

47 This song reminds children in a cheerful way of some of the important things Jesus wants His followers to do. Sing it to the tune of *Did You Ever See a Lassie?* Let children hold hands and sway back and forth gently to the rhythm as they sing.

Let us lo-ve one another,
One another, one another.
Let us lo-ve one another,
For loves comes from God.
We'll love and forgive
And we'll help and we'll share things.
Let us lo-ve one another,
For love comes from God.

48 Have children hold hands with a partner and swing arms as they sing these words to the tune of *London Bridge*.

Love your friends at all times,
All times, all times.
Love your friends at all times,
This will make God happy.

49 Children will enjoy the actions in this song sung to the tune of *Twinkle, Twinkle, Little Star*.

I'm so glad that we can be
　Clap in rhythm
Friends together—you and me.
　Clasp hands, point to friend, then to self
Jesus loves you, this I know
　Point up, tap head
For the Bible tells me so.
　Put open hands together like book
I'm so glad that we can be
　Clap in rhythm
Friends together—you and me.
　Clasp hands, point to friend, then to self

50 Lead preschoolers in this action song sung to *The Farmer in the Dell*.

My good friend taps my back.
My good friend taps my back.
We turn around and then sit down.
My good friend taps my back.

vs.2 My good friend shakes my hand . . .
vs.3 My good friend smiles at me . . .

51 This friend song is sung to *A Tisket, A Tasket*.

I love you, I love you.
   Pat-a-cake with a friend
You are my friend I love you.
I'll share with you
   Grab hands and swing arms
Be kind to you.
You are my friend, I love you.

52 Here's another song about friends to *Twinkle, Twinkle, Little Star*.

I just love to run and play
   Run in place
With my special friends each day.
   Point to another child
When I'm sick or feeling sad,
   Hold stomach; frown
Special friends help make me glad.
   Point to other children; smile
I just love to run and play
   Run in place
With my special friends each day.
   Point to another child

53 For this song, children stand in a circle, holding hands. One child stands in the middle of the circle. Children should walk around while singing the first verse. All verses will be sung to the tune *The Farmer in the Dell*.

Let's tell all our friends, *(Repeat)*
Tell them Jesus loves them so,
Let's tell all our friends,

The child in the middle should choose a friend to also stand in the circle while this next verse is sung. Name of the child choosing should be inserted in blank below.

_____(Child's name) **tells a friend.** *(Repeat)*
_____(Child's name) **tells of Jesus' love.**
_____(Child's name) **tells a friend.**

Child chosen during the above verse should then choose another friend to join in circle. Insert that child's name in verse. The last child to be called into the middle should choose a friend to skip with around the other children while the first verse is repeated.

54 During this song, have children shake hands with each other on the first two lines, then clap hands on the last two. Sing to the tune of *The Farmer in the Dell*.

I'm glad that you're my friend.
Can I be your friend, too?
Let's love each other joyfully,
And love our God, too!

55 Help preschoolers to express thankfulness for their friends and families as they sing this song to *We Wish You a Merry Christmas* (chorus only).

Have children hug each other as they sing:
Let's all lo-ve one another. *(Repeat 2x)*
Just like Jesus said.

Have children join hands as they sing:
Let's all care for one another. *(Repeat 2x)*
Just like Jesus said.

Have children walk in a circle as they sing:
Let's all pray for one another. *(Repeat 2x)*
Just like Jesus said.

56 Sing this song about friends to *Mary Had a Little Lamb*.

Children clap hands as they sing:
Jesus gave us friends to love,
Friends to love, friends to love.
Jesus gave us friends to love,
And He loves us, too.

I love you and you love me,
  Children point to another, then to self
You love me, you love me.
  Point to self
I love you and you love me,
And Jesus loves us, too.
  Point up

Jesus is a friend of mine,
  Point up, then hug self
Friend of mine, friend of mine.
  Hug self
Jesus is a friend of mine,
And I love Him so.

I'll help you and you help me,
  Point to another, then to self
You help me, you help me.
  Point to self
I'll help you and you help me,
We can help each other.

57 Have children hug themselves, rocking back and forth to the rhythm of this song sung to *London Bridge*. On the last line of each verse they will hug another child.

Jesus is my special friend,
Special friend, special friend.
Jesus is my special friend.
And so are you!

I will love my Je-sus,
Je-sus, Je-sus.
I will love my Je-sus.
And I'll love you, too!

58 Do the actions mentioned and sing this partner song to *Row, Row, Row Your Boat*.

Love, love, love your friends,
Help to make them smile.
Give your partner one big hug,
And clap your hands awhile.

YOU AND ME

59 *I'm a Little Teapot* is the tune for these words about growing up.

Now that I am growing up so tall,
  Crouch down, then reach up high
I can jump a rope, and I can bounce a ball.
  Jump, pretend to bounce a ball
I can help my mother and my dad.
Growing up sure makes me glad.
  Reach up high, stand on tiptoes

I am learning how to sing and pray.
  Cup hands around mouth; fold hands
I am learning how to live God's way.
  Point to self, then up
Learning to be helpful, kind, and true,
Is the best thing I can do!
  Clap on the four major beats

60 Sing this growing up song to the tune of *Did You Ever See a Lassie?* Pantomime the activity in each verse.

Would you like to be a grown-up,
A grown-up, a grown-up?
God will help you as you grow up,
But what will you do?

I'll cook in the kitchen,
The kitchen, the kitchen.
God will help me as I grow up,
And that's what I'll do.

vs. 2   I'll work in an office . . .

vs. 3   I'll play with the children . . .

vs. 4   I'll sing praise to Jesus . . .

61 Teach these words to *Ten Little Indians*. Add actions when appropriate.

Trees and flowers—watch them grow.
They need sun and rain you know.
God made many things we see.
He made even you and me!

62 Here's a song about taking care of our pets sung to *Mary Had a Little Lamb*.

I can love my pet today,
Fill his food and water tray.
I will take good care of him.
God will help me.

63 Do these words to the tune of *Itsy Bitsy Spider*.

Sharing is for children;
This is how I know.
    Join hands and walk in a circle
A boy shared his lunch
With Jesus long ago.
    Everyone walk toward center of circle, hands still joined
This made Jesus happy,
And we can please Him, too,
    Drop hands, clap as you back out of center
By sharing with each other
As God would have us do.
    Join hands again and walk in a circle

64 Let pairs of children march around as they sing this sharing song to the tune of *The Mulberry Bush*.

Jesus loves it when we share,
When we share, when we share,
Jesus loves it when we share,
Let's all share today.

65 This song will remind children that it is pleasing to God when we share. Sing to the tune of *Three Blind Mice*.

I like to share. *Clap*
I like to share. *Clap*
I like to share. *Clap*
I like to share. *Clap*
All the things God has given to me,
He wants me to share very joyfully.
By sharing I'm like Jesus wants me to be.
Yes, I like to share. *Clap*
I like to share. *Clap*

66 Lead preschoolers in clapping and singing these words to *This Old Man*.

God wants us
To be fair,
Kind, and helpful,
And to share.
With a great big happy smile,
We can get along.
Clap your hands and sing this song!

67 Children will be reminded that God made them in this next song sung to *Three Blind Mice*.

God made you. God made me.
   Point to someone, then to self
God made you. God made me.
He made my head, and my knees, and my toes.
   Point to body parts mentioned
He made my eyes, and my hands, and my nose.
   Point to body parts mentioned
Because He made me He loves me so.
   Hug self
Yes, God made us all!
   Point up and to others
God made us all!

68 Teach children this fun song to the tune of *The Farmer in the Dell.*

We're growing by leaps and bounds. *(Repeat)*
  Crouch down and jump up
Just like Jesus, we're growing up,
We're growing by leaps and bounds.
  Repeat actions

When Jesus was growing up *(Repeat)*
  Start from a crouching position and straighten up a little
Mary and Joseph took care of Him
When Jesus was growing up.
  Stand up straight

When Jesus was twelve years old *(Repeat)*
  Stand on tip-toes, stretching as tall as possible
He went to the temple to learn about God
When Jesus was twelve years old.

The Spirit came to Him.
  Raise hands up over head and bring back down to touch
    shoulders, like a dove descending on a person
When Jesus went to be baptized,
The Spirit came to Him.
  Repeat hand motions

Just like the fishermen, *(Repeat)*
  Pretend to throw out nets and haul them in
We will come when Jesus calls,
Just like the fishermen.

  Repeat first verse.

69 After each verse of this song, choose a child to act out something that he/she couldn't do when younger. Sing to the tune of *Are You Sleeping?*

Leader (or group): **Are you growing? Are you growing?**
Children: **Yes, I am! Yes, I am!**
Leader (or group): **Show us how you're growing. Show us how you're growing.**
If you can. If you can.

After several times through, close with this verse:

Leader: **Are you growing? Are you growing?**
Children: **Yes, I am! Yes, I am!**
Leader: **As your life keeps going, Who can keep you growing?**
Children: **Jesus can! Jesus can!**

70 Teach these words to *Jesus Loves the Little Children*.

Jesus calls the little children,
    Put hands up to mouth
Calls us all to follow Him.
If we follow Him each day,
    Pretend to march in place
We will never lose our way.
Jesus calls the little children. "Follow Me!"
    Put hands to mouth then motion, "follow me"

71 Children might like to sway as they sing this next song to the tune of *Rock-a-Bye Baby*.

**Who loves the children
Black, white, and red?**
  Pat cheeks
**Who loves the children
Going to bed?**
  Rest hands on head
**Who loves the children
Kneeling to pray?**
  Fold hands in prayer
God our good Father
  Point up
Loves us each day.
  Hug self

**Who loves the children
Both far and near?**
  Indicate left and right
**Who loves the children
Calming their fear?**
  One hand strokes the other
**Who loves the children
Showing the way?**
  March in place
God our good Father
  Point up
Loves us each day.
  Hug self

72 Preschoolers will be encouraged by this next song which reminds them that God is with them when they are afraid. Sing to the tune of *Down by the Station*.

I'm not afraid when Boom! goes the thunder.
Clap hands on "boom"
I'm not afraid when winds blow all around.
Wave hands all around
I remember Jesus is my loving Savior.
Point up; cross arms on chest
Clap, clap, stamp, stamp
I'm His child.

I'm not afraid when I am feeling lonely.
Rest chin in hands
I'm not afraid when Mommy's not around.
Look around
I remember Jesus is my loving Savior.
Point up; cross arms on chest
Clap, clap, stamp, stamp
I'm His child.

73 Children will enjoy the clapping part of this song which is sung to the tune of *Hickory, Dickory, Dock*.

Do you know who loves me?
Clap, clap
Do I know who loves you?
Clap, clap
Our Father God in heaven above
Loves you and loves me, too!
Clap, clap

74

Teach children these words and actions to *Mary Had a Little Lamb*.

Jesus loves you,
  Point up and to others
Yes, He does. *(Repeat 2x)*
  Nod head
Jesus loves me,
  Point up and hug self
Yes, He does.
  Nod head
Jesus, we love You, too.
  Point up

75

Teach these words to *Mary Had a Little Lamb*.

People, people, everywhere
  Point to people around you
Everywhere, everywhere.
We love people everywhere,
  Hug self
Because God made them.

HELPING

76 This is a song that is great to sing while cleaning up. Sing to the tune *Are You Sleeping?*

I am helping, I am helping.
Look at me! Look at me!
Pick up all the paper,
Clean off all the tables,
Nice and neat, nice and neat.

77 Add actions to this song to the tune of *Ten Little Indians*.

These hands, these hands,
These hands are helping hands.
These hands, these hands,
These hands are helping hands.
These hands, these hands,
These hands are helping hands.
They show Jesus' love.

vs. 2 **These feet . . .**

78 Teach this helping song to *Mary Had a Little Lamb*.

Have children pretend to pick up paper scraps as they sing:
I can pick up paper scraps,
Paper scraps, paper scraps.
I can pick up paper scraps.
I'm a helper here.

Have children sing in a whisper:
I can listen quietly,
Quietly, quietly.
I can listen quietly.
I'm a helper here.

HOLIDAYS

79 Teach this Valentine song to *Three Blind Mice*.

Please be my
Valentine.
   Point to self
I'll love you
   Point to another
All the time.
Because Jesus loved me
   Point to self
I love you, too.
   Point to another
Jesus told us to love
For it's right to do.
   Everybody holds hands
Love one another
The whole year through.
So please be my
Valentine.

80 Teach preschoolers this Easter praise song to the tune of *Mary Had a Little Lamb*. Have them clap along.

Jesus is God's special Son,
Special Son, special Son.
Jesus is God's special Son.
He's alive! Let's praise Him!

81

Letting children play musical instruments with this next Easter song will add to the festivities. Sing to the tune of *Old MacDonald Had a Farm.*

Wake up early! Shout and sing.
Jesus is alive!
Flowers bloom, and bells all ring.
Jesus is alive!
So clap your hands;
Stamp your feet.
Here a clap, there a clap;
Everywhere a stamp, stamp.
Wake up early! Shout and sing.
Jesus is alive!

82 Preschoolers will be able to sing about Easter with these words which are sung to *Down by the Station*.

Down in the garden
Early in the morning
Mary saw the cave where
   Hold hands up to eyes as if looking
She thought Jesus lay.
But the stone was gone
And there were angels waiting!
   Point finger as you sing this next line
"Jesus is alive,"
Is what she heard them say.

Mary ran to tell the
Other friends of Jesus
   Pretend to run
That the stone was gone
And Jesus was alive.
Suddenly they saw Him
   Hold hands up to eyes
Standing right beside them.
   Point finger as you sing this next line
He said, "Peace be with you!"
And they were surprised!

83 If you have a special Mother's Day program, invite children to make a circle around their mothers and sing this song to *The Farmer in the Dell*.

You're the best mom in the world. *(Repeat)*
Yes, I really love you so.
You're the best mom in the world.

You take good care of me. *(Repeat)*
Yes, I really love you so.
You take good care of me.

You teach me how to pray. *(Repeat)*
Yes, I really love you so.
You teach me how to pray.

Repeat the first verse.

84 Here's another Mother's Day song to the tune of *Old MacDonald Had a Farm*.

Sing a song about today:
Happy Mother's Day!
  Start to clap hands on the next line
Clap your hands and shout, "Hooray!"
Happy Mother's Day.
So clap your hands,
Shout, "Hooray!"
Here a clap, there a shout,
Everywhere we sing about:
Happy, happy Mother's Day,
Happy Mother's Day!

85 This Father's Day song can be sung by children to their fathers at home or in a program. Sing to *Twinkle, Twinkle, Little Star.*

Daddy, Daddy,
I love you,
  Point to Dad
And the many things you do.
  Put hands on hips
You take care of me each day,
  Point to Dad
Read me books and even play.
  Pretend to read a book
Daddy, Daddy,
I love you.
  Point to Dad
Happy Father's Day to you!

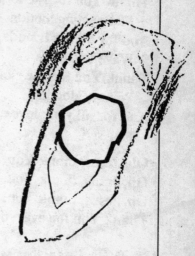

86 This Thanksgiving song is sung to the tune of *Row, Row, Row Your Boat.* After each time of singing, ask children to name something they are thankful for.

Here comes Thanksgiving Day.
Let's all shout, "Hooray!"
Let's thank God for everything
He gives us every day!

87 Here's another Thanksgiving song to the tune of *Jesus Loves Me*.

Thank You for the food I eat,
　Make eating motions
And for all the friends I meet.
　Wave to friends
Thank You for the clothes I wear,
　Point to clothing
And for all your love and care.
　Hug self

Oh, Jesus, thank You.
Oh, Jesus, thank You.
Oh, Jesus, thank You.
Thank You for everything.

88 This last Thanksgiving song is sung to *She'll Be Comin' Round the Mountain When She Comes*.

Let's all clap because we're thankful for our food.
　Spoken: yum, yum. Rub stomach
Let's all clap because we're thankful for our food.
Let's all clap because we're thankful
Let's all clap because we're thankful
Let's all clap because we're thankful for our food.

vs. 2 Let's all clap because we're thankful for our beds . . .
　Spoken: ahhhh. Pretend to be asleep

vs. 3 Let's all clap because we're thankful for our clothes . . .
　Spoken: zzzip. Run thumb from waist to chin